THE AUSTRALIAN CHILDREN'S OMNIBUS

POEMS BY DAN VALLELY
ILLUSTRATED BY YVONNE PERRIN

CHILD & ASSOCIATES
AN ALL-AUSTRALIAN PUBLISHER

BOOK ONE

Possum One
The Outback
Rocket Ship

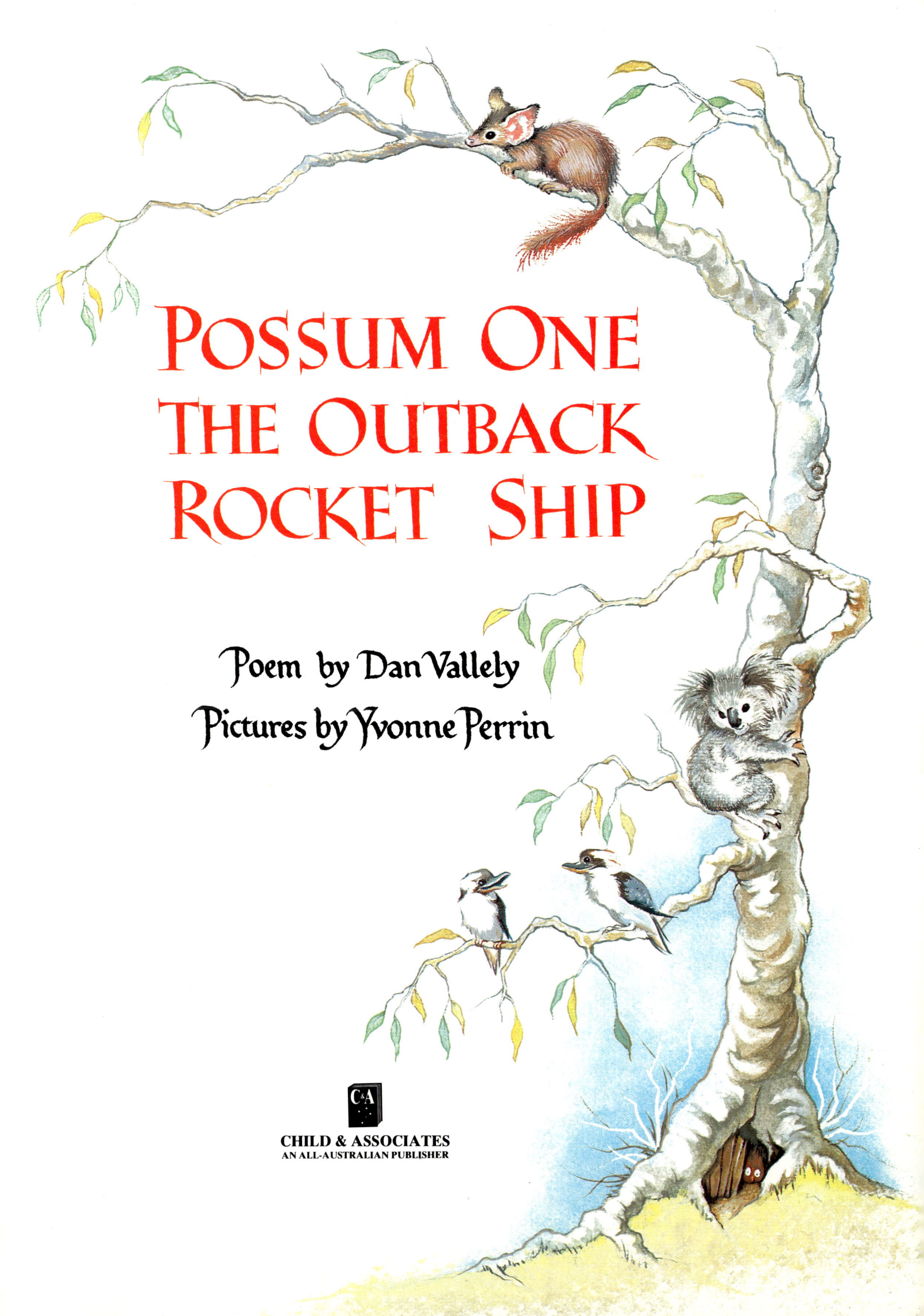

Possum One
The Outback
Rocket Ship

Poem by Dan Vallely

Pictures by Yvonne Perrin

CHILD & ASSOCIATES
AN ALL-AUSTRALIAN PUBLISHER

It was a Monday afternoon
On the twenty-third of June
When in Possum Creek a strange event occurred.
Striding into town
In his mortar-board and gown
Came Professor Cockatoo, that learned bird.

Ed Galah who was related,
Upon conferring, indicated
That his cousin was the bearer of great news,
Which he would gladly tell to all
In the Possum Creek Town Hall,
Post-haste for there was little time to lose.

Within seconds all were seated
And the Professor warmly greeted
As he rose to get proceedings underway.
"Friends and neighbours," he began,
"I have a most exciting plan
Which I will now unfold before you if I may.

"I have built a rocket ship
Which will be leaving on a trip
Very shortly, but I have a need of you.
A number of your best
Must face their greatest test
And volunteer to be my rocket crew."

In an hour the recruits
Were putting on their suits,
Wally Wombat, Platypus and Ed Galah,
Big Red Kangaroo
And Peter Possum too,
All bound for some enticing distant star.

They could feel the tension mount
As they began the final count,
Two seconds, one and then a mighty roar,
As they rose into the sky
They sighed a nervous sigh
And hoped that they would see their homes once more.

Then with a rolling motion
As if upon an ocean
She veered away from her intended course.
Back towards the ground
She came with dreadful sound
And frightened Tommy Numbat's trotting horse.

Once more on level plane
She roared down Emu Lane
And swept the tiles from Tim Koala's house.
The crew, in disarray,
Watched in great dismay
As the wayward rocket chased Marsupial Mouse.

Through the bakery she ploughed
Enveloping the crowd
With a coat of flour to everyone's surprise.
And Mrs Tiger Snake
Was knocked into the lake
After being struck by several peanut pies.

She screamed left at Dingo Road
And rammed the posh abode
Of the Honourable George Goanna, man of leisure,
Then carved a gaping path
Right through his marble bath
Whilst he was in it, much to his displeasure.

On and on she sped,
As the Mayor stood hands on head,
For the only house still standing was his own.
Then her engine coughed and died
And as His Worship cried
She dropped upon his cottage like a stone.

As we came upon the scene
Where the Mayoral house had been
The rocket crew were stumbling from the wreck.
With luck that was amazing
Injuries were limited to grazing
And a rather minor case of cricked neck.

Thus the saga ended
In a manner not intended
And, even though disaster dogged their trip,
They raised a statue to it
And the gallant crew who flew it,
    Possum One,
        the Outback
            Rocket Ship.

BOOK TWO

Professor Cockatoo's Amazing Weather Dust

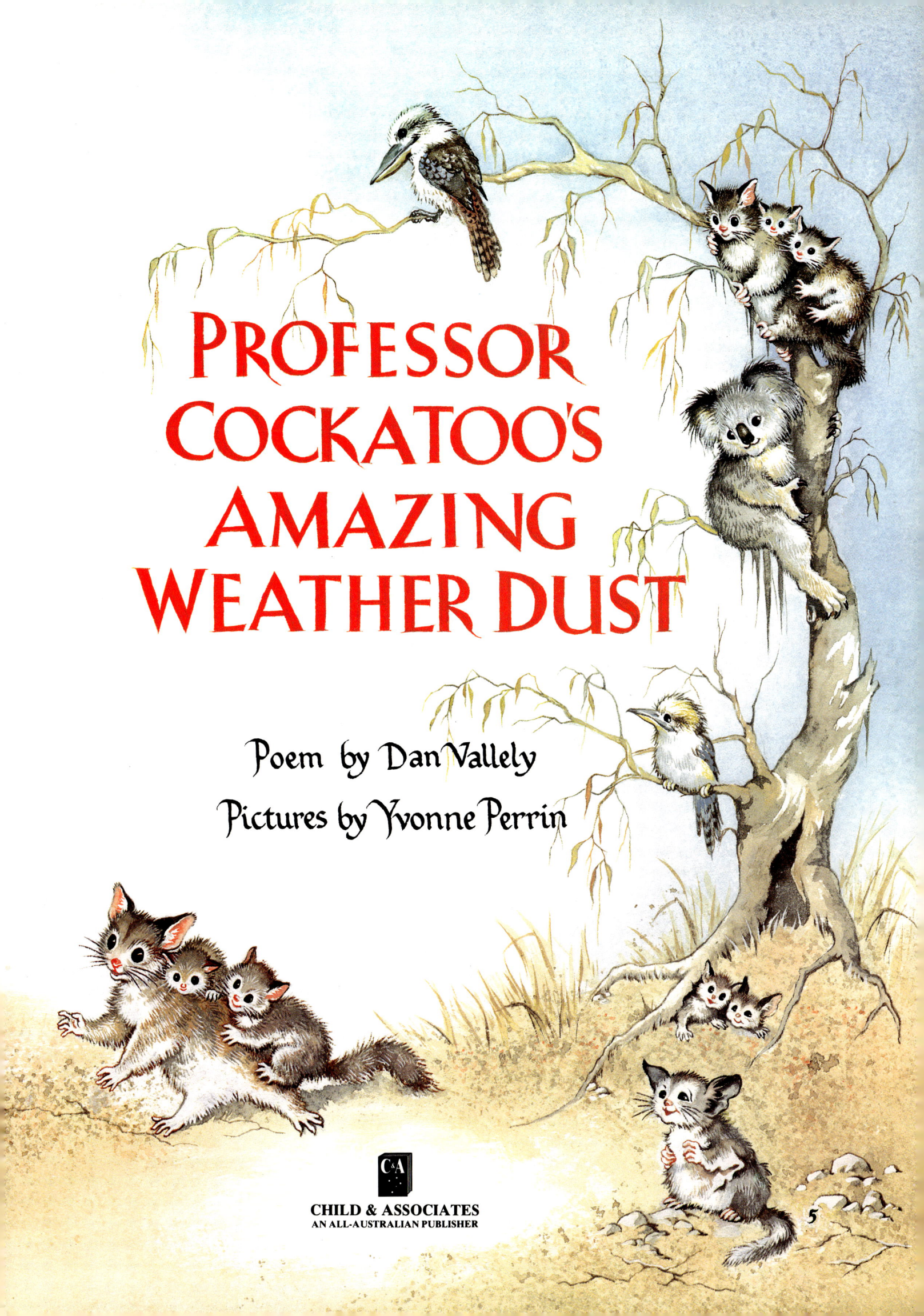

Professor Cockatoo's Amazing Weather Dust

Poem by Dan Vallely

Pictures by Yvonne Perrin

CHILD & ASSOCIATES
AN ALL-AUSTRALIAN PUBLISHER

It was spring in Possum Creek
But the future seemed quite bleak,
For a cruel drought held sway upon the land.
The lake was drying fast
And they knew it wouldn't last.
In short a dreadful crisis was at hand.

Tom Echidna trusty Mayor,
With rare judgement did declare,
"There is one whose brilliant mind may hold the clue,
To save us from disaster,
Send for Possum Creek's headmaster,
That gifted bird, Professor Cockatoo."

Unknown to friends and neighbours,
That wise scholar in his labours
On that problem had been working day and night.
And had, as it transpired,
In the end though greatly tired,
Made a substance which might save them from their plight.

The following day at noon
Aboard a great balloon
Stepped the gallant band who'd vowed to save the day.
Whilst the good Professor fussed,
Checking bags of weather dust,
They untied the rope and slowly sailed away.

Big Red Kangaroo, as planned,
Took charge of ballast sand.
Ed Galah stood by a cannon of great size.
Wally Wombat steered the craft
And Peter Possum stationed aft,
With Platypus, kept watch with anxious eyes.

They fired a practice round
To ensure the gun was sound,
But, alas, the Flying Doctor was close by.
With his aircraft blown to shreds,
He wrecked several chicken sheds
And crash-landed in Tim Wallaby's pigsty.

The crew, quite sad of face,
Filled the gun with half a case
Of weather dust and lit the fuse with care.
A mighty boom resounded
And the creatures stood dumbfounded
As a mass of swirling snowflakes filled the air.

The blizzard still increasing
Showed little sign of ceasing.
Icy breezes lashed the bushland folk.
Where the sun had just been blazing
They gaped at scenes amazing
As the bush lay white beneath a wintry cloak.

Another boom much louder
Indicated extra powder
Had been used to try to rectify the mess.
The blizzard, changing form,
Became a wild electric storm
But as for rain, they'd still had no success.

This time, the gun, reloaded
With a mite too much, exploded
Scattering the crew both far and wide.
Cockatoo and Ed Galah
Were the luckiest by far
And flew away with little hurt but pride.

Platypus with graceful arc
Came down inside the park
Upon a hornet's nest, as fate decreed.
The occupants of course
Protested with such force
That he departed shortly after at great speed.

Peter Possum somersaulted
Until his progress halted
At the dairy in a tub of cottage cheese.
Wally Wombat, always brave,
Caused a mini-tidal wave
As he hit Lake Wongi, backwards if you please.

Big Red, reluctant flyer,
Struck the Town Hall spire
And quickly tumbled off towards the ground,
To land with doubtful luck
Upon the garbage truck
Which was passing at the moment on its round.

Their tribulations ended
With the heroes well attended
In the hospital, a sick and sorry lot.
But wondrous pouring rain
Soon washed away their pain
And exhausted, each slept soundly in his cot.

Thus the gallant few,
With their share of luck it's true,
Put an end to Possum Creek's worst ever drought,
With good old Aussie grit,
They stood the test and mastered it.
We shall hear from them again, I have no doubt.

BOOK THREE

THE GREAT POSSUM CREEK BUSH FIRE

Dedication:
For our son, Kieran Joseph
Dan & Rhonda Vallely

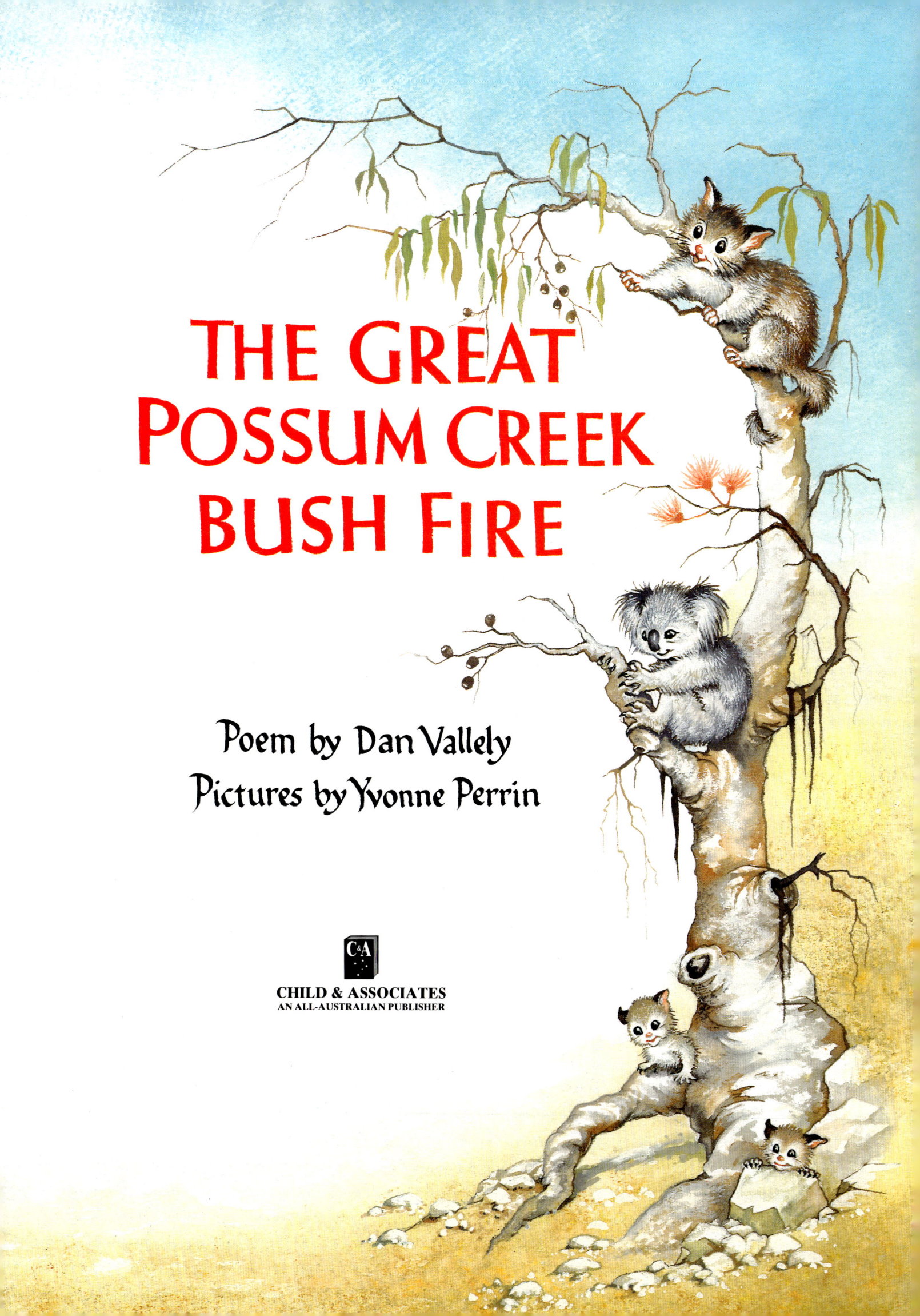

THE GREAT POSSUM CREEK BUSH FIRE

Poem by Dan Vallely
Pictures by Yvonne Perrin

CHILD & ASSOCIATES
AN ALL-AUSTRALIAN PUBLISHER

It was a sleepy Sunday morning
Just a little after dawning
And the town of Possum Creek was calm and still.
As the animals were stirring
A disaster was occurring
As a flame burst forth upon a distant hill.

Big Red Kangaroo on rising
Thought it quite surprising
That the smell of smoke lay heavy on the air.
For the council of the shire
Had placed a total ban on fire
And they'd all been warned to take the utmost care.

As he ran into the clearing
The event that he'd been fearing
Was an awful fact, as he could plainly tell.
For a wall of flames was burning
And was very quickly turning
All the bush to ashes, just near Wombats' Well.

It was clear Big Red was worried
As with frantic haste he scurried
To the firehouse to set off the alarm.
Within seconds bells were ringing,
And the firetruck was bringing
All the volunteers to fight for Wombats' farm.

Peter Possum did the driving
And they saw upon arriving
That the flames had very nearly won the day.
They were licking round the stable
And the youngest wombat, Mabel,
Was leading all the horses far away.

The fire chief was Ed Galah,
Who drove an extra special car
Whose klaxon guaranteed to wake the dead,
As he drove up, klaxon blaring,
Very dignified of bearing,
They'd already lost the fodder storage shed.

Ed Galah, with cool precision,
Made his vital first decision
As he put the dingo brothers on the pumps.
Two numbats manned the hoses
And demolished several roses
And a beehive, causing many painful lumps.

By the time their aim was better
There was nothing any wetter
Than the volunteers, a sorry dripping bunch.
But their spirit was unbroken,
No faint-hearted words were spoken
Even though they hadn't time to stop for lunch.

Slowly they were winning
For the ranks of flames were thinning
And finally the house was safe at last.
But the clean-up was aborted
When a sharp-eyed crow reported
That the flames on Possum Creek were closing fast.

So with bells a-madly clanging
And equipment all a-banging
They sped back to town to start the fight anew.
From atop the fire station
They then gazed with consternation
On the blackened fields where corn and wheat once grew.

Tom Echidna, who was mayor,
Ever keen to do his share
Displayed to all his loyalty and grit.
With a flourish brave and bold,
He threw off his chain of gold
And proudly marched away to do his bit.

As the ring of flames came closer,
Billy Platypus, the grocer,
Shouted, "Men, although the water's running low,
Because of next week's picnic races
I've bought fifty dozen cases
Of the finest lemonade, as you all know.

"And if vigorously shaken
Unless I'm much mistaken,
As extinguishers they'll really fit the bill."
And so with scant decorum
They raced back to Billy's store-room
That lay behind the old abandoned mill.

They stood, bottles at the ready,
As the fire chief said "Steady",
With courage rare they made their final stand.
And though the blaze approached them
And very nearly poached them
The bushland heroes kept it well in hand.

By the time that they were finished
The flames were quite diminished
And relief was plain on every face in town.
Twelve hours, they had fought it
And as sure as I report it
With exhaustion every creature then fell down.

Now if you ever spend a week
Down there with friends at Possum Creek
The locals will be happy to relate
How as the flames were leaping higher
They bravely soda-popped the fire
And in the end just beat it by a crate.

Published by
Child & Associates Publishing Pty Ltd
5 Skyline Place, Frenchs Forest, NSW, Australia, 2086
A wholly owned Australian publishing company
First Omnibus Edition 1986
Second Omnibus Edition 1988
Paperback Edition 1989

Possum One: The Outback Rocket Ship
Poem © Dan Vallely 1981
Illustrations © Yvonne Perrin 1981

Professor Cockatoo's Amazing Weather Dust
Poem © Dan Vallely 1983
Illustrations © Yvonne Perrin 1983

The Great Possum Creek Bush Fire
Poem © Dan Vallely 1988
Illustrations © Yvonne Perrin 1988

Printed in Hong Kong by Everbest Printing Co. Ltd
National Library of Australia Card Number and
ISBN 0 86777 103 8
All rights reserved. No part of this publication may be
reproduced, stored in a retrieval system, or transmitted
in any form or by any means, electronic, mechanical,
photocopying, recording, or otherwise, without the
prior permission in writing of the publisher.